COLOR TEST PAGE

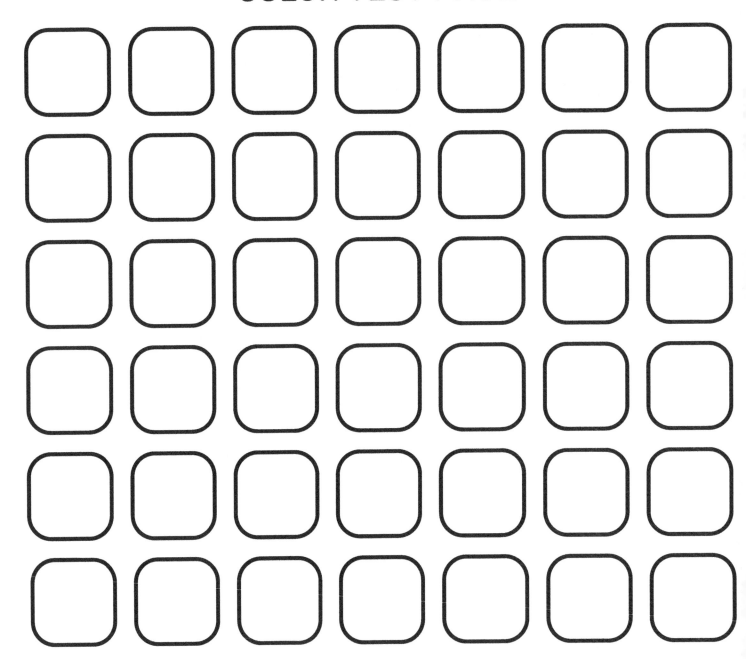

Copyright © 2023 by Zoe James
All Rights Reserved
No part of this book may be reproduced or transmitted in any form or by any means whatsoever without express written permission from the author, except in the case of brief quotations embodied in critical articles and reviews.

Made in the USA
Monee, IL
29 June 2023

38047920R00044